Poetic Injustice

Copyright © 2022 BFF Publishing House, LLC

Printed in the United States of America

Email address: bff@bffpublishinghouse.com

Website: www.bffpublishinghouse.com

ISBN: 978-1-7377800-6-9

Disclaimer: This book is the author's personal, non-fictional story. Every account in the book is true, and the events are portrayed to the best of the author's memory. While all the stories in this book are true, names and identifying details were eliminated to protect the privacy of the people involved. The authors do not assume and hereby disclaims any liability to any party for any loss, damage, emotional distress, or disruption as a result of the book content.

Printed in the United States of America. All rights reserved under international Copyright Law.

Contents and/or cover may not be reproduced in whole or in any form without the express written consent of the Publisher, except by a reviewer, who may quote brief passages in connection with a review for a magazine or newspaper.

BFF Publishing House is a Limited Liability Corporation dedicated wholly to the appreciation and publication of books for children and adults for the advancement of diversification in literature.

For more information on publishing contact:

Antionette Mutcherson, MBA at
bff@bffpublishinghouse.com
Website: bffpublishinghouse.com
Published in the United States by
BFF Publishing House
Atlanta, Georgia First Edition, 2022

Dedication

This book is dedicated to my father, Anthony Mutcherson, whom I lost during the creation of this book. I miss you tremendously. I can still feel your love from Heaven and I pray that you can still feel mine.

To ALL of the victims of social injustice, police brutality, and inequality. We live to honor you. You will never be forgotten.

Ahmaud Arbery
Aidan Ellison
Aiyana Stanley-Jones
Akai Gurley
Alberta Odell Jones
Alberta Spruill
Alesia Thomas
Alteria Woods
Alton Sterling
Amadou Diallo
Amir Brooks
Anthony Dwain Lee
Anthony McClain
Antwon Rose Jr.
Atatiana Jefferson
Aura Rosser
Barry Gedeus
Bettie Jones
Botham Jean
Breonna Taylor
Calvin Horton Jr.
Cameron Tillman
Casey Goodson Jr.
Charleena Lyles
Charles "Chop" Roundtree Jr.
Christian Taylor

Cletis Williams
Corey Jones
Corey Stingley
Cornelius Fredericks
Damian Daniels
Daniel Prude
Danroy "DJ" Henry Jr.
Darius Simmons
Darius Tarver
Darnesha Harris
Darrien Hunt
Darrius Stewart
David Joseph
David McAtee
DeAunta Farrow
Deborah Danner
Deion Fludd
Dijon Kizzee
Dion Johnson
Dion Johnson
Dominique Clayton
Dorian Harris
Eleanor Bumpurs
Elijah McClain
Elton Hayes
Emmett "Bobo" Till
Eric Garner
Eugene Ellison
Ezell Ford
Fred Hampton
Freddie Gray
Gabriella Nevarez
George Floyd
George Stinney Jr.
Gynnya McMillen
Jaleel Medlock

Jamel Floyd
James "Juju" Scurlock
James Byrd Jr.
James Earl Chaney
Janisha Fonville
Jaquyn O'Neill Light
Jassmine McBride
Jimmie Lee Jackson
John Crawford III
John Earl Reese
Jonathan Price
Jordan Davis
Jordan Edwards
Julian Alexander
Julian Lewis
Kalief Browder
Kamal Flowers
Kathryn Johnston
Kayla Moore
Kendra James
Kendrick Johnson
Kenneth Chamberlain Sr.
Kimani Gray
Laquan McDonald
LaVena Johnson
Lawrence Allen
Louis Allen
Malissa Williams
Margaret LaVerne Mitchell
Marvin Parker
Mary Mitchell
Maurice Abisdid-Wagner
Maurice Gordon
Medgar Evers
Michael Brown
Michelle Cusseaux

Miciah Lee
Miriam Carey
Natasha McKenna
Nicholas Heyward Jr.
Oluwatoyin Salau
Oscar Grant
Pamela Turner
Patrick Warren
Philando Castile
Quawan "Bobby" Charles
Quintonio LeGrier
Rayshard Brooks
Reika Boyd
Renisha McBride
Ricky Byrdsong
Robert Forbes
Robert Ricks
Sandra Bland
Sean Bell
Sgt. James Brown
Shantel Davis
Sharon Walker
Shelly Frey
Shereese Francis
Stephon Clark
Steven Taylor
Tamir Rice
Tanisha Anderson
Tarika Wilson
Timothy Stansbury Jr.
Tony McDade
Trayvon Martin
Tywanza Sanders
Walter Wallace Jr.
Willie Ray Banks
Xzavier Hill
Yvette Smith

Acknowledgements

To the Authors:
You all are a consistent source of inspiration to me. Thank you for breathing life into this project. You all made my dream come true... again. My dream is to publish the most children who share my same life experiences, my hopes, my struggles, my power, and my heritage; you are the antidote and you are not alone. Look at us: Here we are, over 200 Black American children authors strong through this initiative.

To the Parents:
Thank you for entrusting us with your children's stories. We could not have done this without your unwavering support.

To the BFF Publishing House Team:
You are the epitome of my personal mantra—"God sends angels." God knew that I needed you and He led us to each other ever so divinely. Thank you from the bottom of my heart.
Riel, the world's best editor and assistant—you are my literary soulmate. Thank you for existing, and for ALWAYS being a positive force in both my personal and professional life.

To my Family and Friends:
Thank you for praying with me and for me, especially on the tough days. Special thanks to my mother, Cannella Mutcherson-Jefferies, Jett Lemon, Dr. Asha Brewer and the Temple FIT family, Baconton Missionary Baptist Church, Lynn Beckom, Stephanye Watts, Stephen Churn, Carlos Scott, Jimmie Starkes, Celeste Clark, Brandon Martin, Rudy Simpson, Angela Simpson, and Kathryn Stanley. You all were the boots on the ground aiding us to get the word out and getting the kids to sign up.

To our Donors and Sponsors:
　　　Thank you for your kind contributions. It really does take a village. With your financial support, we were able to provide writing resources to and publish 100 more Black children free of charge.

Darius Alvira
LaTonya Bell
Makisha Cameron, MBA
Stephen Churn (I Am College 501c3)
Renisha Gibbs
Lexie Mutherson, MBA (LCM Logistics)
The Jefferies Family (Vandella's Dream)
La'Dreauna Johnson (LaceeJProductions)
Teirra Jordan
Nichelle Joyner
Carruthers Kimberly
Gena Kimbrough
Leia Mandeville
Mathew Massaquoi
Treemonisha McGee
Cecile McKnight
Mikia Muhammad
Shay Myrick
Marquita Priester (marquitapriester.com)
Danielle Roberson
Richele Robinson, Pharm D
Naijha Wright-Brown (The Land of Kush, VeganSoul Bistro)
Stephanye Watts

A Poem from the Publisher

ANTIDOTE

When they try to test your confidence
and lie to you about them being dominant,
Show Them Who You Are.

When they doubt your brilliance because they prejudge you,
don't let their ignorance destroy you.
Show Them Who You Are.

When they rip pages from school books to revise their so-called history,
seek the truth of your melanated mystery.
Show Them Who You Are.

When they define beauty with the likeness of European creatures,
remind them that your ancestors' natural beauty is still the most sought-after feature.
Show Them Who You Are.

When they use their systemic privilege to hold you back,
never forget that those who came before you live inside you.
There's nothing that you lack.
Show Them Who You Are.

When they make you feel like it's easier to just quit,
reach deep down within, push through the pain, and ignite your grit.
Show Them Who You Are.

When they bully you and then cry victim,
arm yourself with the power of prayer, inner peace, and judicial wisdom.
Show Them Who You Are.

Who Are You?

You are illustrious.
You are magisterial.
You are glorious.
You are miraculous.
You are anomalous.
You are benevolent.
You are the antidote.

Antionette Mutcherson, MBA
CEO/Founder of BFF Publishing House, LLC

A Poem from the Editor

All for What?

Little Black girl
with your bold lips and spiraled curls,
do you not know
that you're a gift to this world?

Little Black boy
with your plastic gun as a toy,
please be careful.
In an instant, your entire life can be destroyed

by the stereotypes
society has set in stone
for little Black children like you.

Darling, oh, darling,
it breaks my heart, too—
and all for what?
Oh, darling,
if only I had a clue.

Strong Black woman,
I am you.
I see you.
I fight for you.

Calloused Black man,
I love you.
I see you.
I fight for you.

I fight for us,
and all for what?
We did not ask for this—
did not ask for
our ancestors to be shackled
did not ask for
centuries of oppression
did not ask for
unjust incarceration
did not ask
to be born
Black.

Did anyone ever realize that?

But alas,
we are little Black girls
and we are little Black boys
with bold lips and kinky curls
who just want to play as cowboys.

We are Black men
and we are Black women
who make a way
day after day
in this cruel world that we live in.

We are here
and we are fighting
and all… for what?

Remember that we never once asked.

— Riel Felice
Editor of BFF Publishing House, LLC

Contents

Dedication	5
Acknowledgement	9
A Poem from the Publisher	11
A Poem from the Editor	13
Black and White, Dark and Light	23
GEORGE FLOYD	24
Pillars of Equality	25
Quit Denying Your Privilege	26
I Love My Black Skin	28
Black = Excellence	29
I See the World	30
The Truth	31
Black Me You Can't See	32
Life in a Black-and-White World	33
I Am Excellence	35
Police Brutality	36
Why Me?	37
I Matter	38
My Black Family	39
I Love Being Black	40
One and the Same	41
Why?	42

Disconnection	43
Brown Skin Girl	45
How People Should Be Treated	46
I AM BLACK	47
Black Is Power	48
We Will Rise	49
Does My Life Hurt You?	50
This Is Who I Am	51
A Blessing	53
Black Is Me	54
My Future	55
How I Wish	57
I Am a Queen	58
My Life	59
How's Life Been?	60
Afros	61
Equal Rights	62
Dream	63
House on a Hill	64
Social Injustice	65
Jailah's Thoughts	66
This Is Me	67
Those Two	68
Racism	69
Life's Loneliness	70

I Am	71
I Wish	72
Who Am I?	73
Hate in Their Hearts	74
Black for the WIN!	75
My Skin	76
Black Lives Matter	77
I Am Black and Proud	78
If You Like It or Not	79
My Dream	80
Young Black Man	81
Racism in America	82
The Evolution of My Brown Skin	83
A Terrible Thing	84
As Dark as Can Be	85
In A Better World	86
I Am Powerful	87
Mama	88
Brown Skin Girl	89
Brown Skin Boy	90
Our Power!	91
Black Strength	92
CRAIG	93
KAHLAN	94

Black Is Great	95
My Feelings on My Skin	96
BLM	97
Up We Go!	98
I Am Loved	99
I Am Black	100
Pretty Black Flower	101
Racism Hurts	102
Being Black Is Awesome	103
Black Boy, Black Boy	104
Target	105
AFRO	106
Our Voice	107
I Love Being Black	108
JUDITH: Justice for Everyone	109
DURDEN	110
I Have Faith	111
Things I've Seen	112
Hard Work Unlocks Your Talent	113
I Am Love	114
I Am Amazing	115
Life	116
Black Is Everything	117
Young and Black	118

Skin	119
Why Does It Matter?	120
Black Women	121
Being Black	122
My Feeling	123
I'm Angry	124
I Will Be the Change	125
I'm Not Afraid	126
My People	127
I Am Grateful	128
I Love My Hair	129
Multifaceted	130
Wouldn't You Hate?	131
The Scared Twelve-Year-Old	132
What Makes Me Special?	133
Biography of Antionette Mutcherson, MBA	134
Biography of Riel Felice	136

1. Black and White, Dark and Light

Black and white,
dark and light,
I experience social discrimination
when nothing is wrong with my skin of the night.

Inky and bright,
dark and light.
Discriminated against—why?
Due to my civil rights?

You treat me inferior,
as if we are so different,
as if we are diseased, just as blight.
You simply choose to ignite.

We could come as one.
Why choose to discriminate?
Hear me out; let's communicate.

Wari Ogoun II, 12
Atlanta, Georgia

2. George Floyd

George Floyd, the spark of a commanding movement—

Empowering others like me to speak so highly in my people's favor;

Omitting all negativity, and seeking justice for those who were also taken;

Restoring strength and will in those who continue to fight and believe;

Giving our communities hope for change and light for a new day;

Envisioning a better and safer world, where the thought, *We don't matter*

Fails to exist, and a world where social injustice no longer holds us;

Leaving us, the Black community, inspired and unfearful of what's ahead.

Only then can we relax, but for now, we use our voices to rise above, because

Yesterday's past can be a new tomorrow, and that past will never

Define us.

Sean Ouattara, 17
Duluth, Georgia

3. Pillars of Equality

I survive with fear on my back
weighing me down and
pulling at me because I'm Black.
Though, as hard as it
may be to see, we all
deserve equality.

I refuse to give in because
My Young Life Matters.

Peter Richards, 14
Douglasville, Georgia

4. Quit Denying Your Privilege

Me:
Box braids flowing down my back with a little tint of brown at the end.
Dark brown eyes you might mistake for black.
Straight A student,
featured with my smooth, brown-colored skin.

Her:
Long, blond hair, which would always be in her face
because of the constant kisses from the wind.
Behind it lurked her light brown eyes that you wouldn't mistake for black.
Freckles dappled all around her face.
She was crazy—not about her school work, but about the boys.
Of course I couldn't forget her colored skin.
Yeah, that's where the privilege comes from,

She never really liked me.
I didn't know why.
She did horrible things to me, but I was the one who would always be in trouble.
What? Why?

She hit me.

I hit her back.

Suspended.

She stole my belongings.

I went to address her about it, but she told twelve that it was vice versa.

Arrested.

She had the weapon in her hand.

I was unarmed and I complied.

Dead.

But you claim you don't have privilege?

H'ermani Watts, 13
Atlanta, Georgia

5. I Love My Black Skin

I love my Black smile;
I love my Black mind.

I love my Black God;
I let my Black shine.

I love my Black future;
I love my Black past.

I love my Black music;
I love my Black swag.

I love my Black friends;
I love my Black team.

I love my Black skin!
I love my Black dreams.

Parker Simpson, 7
Atlanta, Georgia

6. Black - Excellence

Black has style.

Black has melanin.

Black has curls, locs, braids, waves, twists.

Black has perseverance.

Black has music.

Black has strength.

Black is power.

Black is excellence.

They fear Black, for we have what they don't.

Jaunte Joiner, 12
Atlanta, Georgia

7. I See the World

I see the world as hate.
I see the world as despair.
I see the world as people being treated unfairly.
I see the world as people hurting others.

But looking in a different lens,
I see the world as wonder.
I see the world as hope.
I see the world as peace.
I see the world as joy.
I see the world as people treating others fairly.
I see people making the world a better place.

Thomas Tedder II, 14
Jacksonville, Florida

8. The Truth

Society, society, what is the truth?

I see you spit those spiteful lies

as you watch the people who trusted you die.

Now, I know that might sound sad, but that's the truth

of those cruel lies.

Ava Gaines, 12
Atlanta, Georgia

9. Black Me You Can't See

Black me, you can't see

when I walk in the store and people see my braids.

I'm unique,

and I say I am.

Black me, you can't see

I am thinking about slavery.

Wow! My people are stronger than you know.

Black me, you can't see

we are all the same, just different colors.

Let my people go free.

Naiyima Warner, 11
Tallahassee, Florida

10. Life in a Black-and-White World

As a Black person in America,
and young, I don't really have
a lot to say about my life.
But in the years that I have lived,
I have experienced a lot of
things that have to do with Black people.

In 2020, a person named George Floyd was 32.
He was being held down to the ground,
being suffocated for ten minutes straight,
saying he could not breathe,
and the police officer did not stop until he died.

And now, to this day,
they sentenced the police officer
to twenty-one-and-a-half years in prison.
But George Floyd's family is doing good to this day.

What I go through at school every day
is white people trying to say the N-word daily.

They think they're Black.

They think just because they have one Black friend,

they get something called a "free Black pass."

They think that gives them the right and power to say something,

even the N-word.

The N-word dates to 1837,

when slaves were being called that.

So, nowadays,

when someone say the N-word,

or something related to that,

they are just calling themselves

or other people

"slaves,"

"cotton pickers,"

"porch monkeys,"

and other unprofessional words.

Proceed in life and do not be a hater.

Nasyh Williams, 12
Jacksonville, FL

11. I Am Excellence

Even though people may not see,

I am made of excellence.

Even though people hate,

I am excellence.

Don't shade me; my skin is excellence, too.

I AM EXCELLENCE.

Adisa Luqman, 12
Atlanta, Georgia

12. Police Brutality

People are getting shot for no reason.

We get accused of stealing, but we're not.

Little children get shot, too.

Police brutality makes me angry. White people

are killing us for no reason, just like

George Floyd, Breonna Taylor, and Trayvon Martin.

I'll know when racism is over when

police stop killing us.

Tyler Greg, 11
Tallahassee, Florida

13. Why Me?

Walking out of the door with a red hoodie and Jordans on, a young Black man risks his life to catch a school bus. Looking cautiously behind me, in fear of being caught jaywalking, fearful of what I will be perceived as...

Can't get locs—"You'll look like a thug," they say, but who is "they," really?

Society? Me? My parents? My elders? My friends? I don't know.

"I wanna stretch my hands and feel no walls. I wanna stand as tall as I possibly can and be as far from the ceiling as possible. I'm chasing freedom." — SAINt JHN

That's how I feel. Have you ever heard a quote that touches you so deeply that you're speechless? Yeah, that's how I feel now.

Expressing myself is my only real desire, because who knows what the Black, five-foot-eight kid wearing a red hoodie and Jordans, crossing the street to catch a school bus really knows—or, more so, who cares? When will you value me enough to care? When I'm dead and gone?

Christian Elahee, 16
Atlanta, Georgia

14.) Matter

I matter.

Not the color of my skin; not the texture of my hair.

I matter.

Not the neighborhood I live in or the school I attend.

I matter.

Not the clothes I wear or the way I speak.

I matter.

The smile on my face is like the sun rising and shining on a new day.

That's me every day.

We matter.

Olivia George, 7
Duluth, Georgia

15. My Black Family

My Black family is important to me.

They are the love that I see:

My big brother is fast,

my mother is smart,

my father is strong,

my baby brother is cool.

And me?

I am a future chef.

All Black families are special!

Justus Hutchinson, 8
Atlanta, Georgia

16. I Love Being Black

I love hip-hop.

I love my culture.

I love my family history.

I love that Black comes in different shades.

I love that I have a mom.

I love my hair.

I love how tall I am.

I love that I have a house.

I love that my family LOVES me.

I love my life!

I love myself!

Maheyla Bennett, 8
East Orange, New Jersey

17. One and the Same

We are people—

God's people.

We are supposed to care for one another,

raise one another,

and fix each other's crowns,

not murder each other with our words.

Be kind. It counts.

It counts because we all need love.

It counts because we are one and the same.

Jada Lemon, 14
Atlanta, Georgia

18. Why?

Why are police rude?

Why do I get scared of them?

Why not protect us?

Paris Giles, 11
Atlanta, Georgia

19. Disconnection

"We should tell history like the old days."
That's what you say.
Trying to tell the story one way,
knowing that it can impact us
negatively.

"Make America great again."
Oh, you're lying, my friend.
You and I have different plans.

I help speak for my community;
we're people of unity.
You sit in your chair and count bills
despite how everyone feels.
You defund hospitals;
our population gets little.

You're a fool,
and it's cruel.
We just want peace and equality,
but we have a disconnection

'cause you're going in a different
direction.

The government is corrupted,
but no one wants to get busted
or cares that our history was interrupted.

Reagan McGill, 16
Atlanta, Georgia

20. Brown Skin Girl

I am pretty.

I like ice cream.

I am strong.

I love my brown skin!

Ma'Loni Ponder, 6
Tallahassee, Florida

21. How People Should Be Treated

People should be treated equally.

Police should not harm peaceful people without good reason.

Justice should be provided to all races and types of people.

Black people should not kill their own kind for money, drugs, or gang stuff.

Black people should not harm their own skin kind.

Instead, they should help each other become better.

Justice needs to be provided to every human.

And police brutality has to stop.

My skin is beautiful,

and so is yours.

Everyone's skin is beautiful.

Noah Grant, 12
Jacksonville, Florida

22. I AM BLACK

Imaginative—I love to use my imagination.

Amazing—I have amazing talents.

Marvelous—I am an extraordinary person.

Brave—I take lots of risks.

Loyal—I stay there for my friends and family.

Appreciative—I appreciate what I get.

Careful—I make sure my friends and family are safe.

Kind—I respect my family and friends.

Brylan Thaxter, 11
Atlanta, Georgia

23. Black Is Power

I love being Black.

It makes me feel confident.

It makes me feel like a queen!

My hair is beautiful.

My smile is bright.

My skin is perfect for me!

Loving all of me is my power, because being Black is powerful!

Kylah Hollingsworth, 8
Smyrna, Georgia

24. We Will Rise

We work and work every day,
but our talents are still not on display.
We try our hardest to fit in,
but we still can't find a way to win.

We will rise through the struggle.
We will have to hustle and hustle
just to be on top.

We must fight the burdens with a brass knuckle.

Caleb Allen, 14
Jacksonville, Florida

25. Does My Life Hurt You?

Does my life hurt you?

Does my dark skin hurt you?

Does my curly Afro hurt you?

Does my unique style hurt you?

Does my knowledge hurt you?

Does my strength hurt you?

Does my Black history hurt you?

Do my special talents hurt you?

Does my Black girl magic hurt you?

Marlei Jackson, 12
Atlanta, Georgia

26. This Is Who I Am

I am Black.

I am proud.

I am strong.

I am unstoppable.

I am patient.

I am understanding.

I am a king.

I am outstanding.

I am athletic.

I am tall.

I am skinny.

I am respectful.

I am Alvin Garrett.

I am a young Black man.

I play sports and I do what I can.

That is who I am.

Alvin Garrett, 12
Atlanta, Georgia

27. A Blessing

Being Black is a blessing—

a blessing that can take us far,

a blessing that will allow us to make a change.

Change is what we need.

Needs are something we feed on.

Blessing after blessing;

a blessing is what we are.

We have come far from what we were.

What we were has depicted how much we need change.

Change is what we need.

Safani Slaton, 13
Atlanta, Georgia

28. BLACK Is Me

Being me is great!

Love is Black.

Act Black,

Caught in the experience of being Black.

Keep being Black!

Christopher Dalton, 13
Atlanta, Georgia

29. My Future

Crimson red blood

smeared the steaming pavement.

Red and blue lights in the distance,

my lifeless body lay still—

WAIT.

NO,

not entirely lifeless.

I can't leave—

not yet.

I haven't been the first Black person

to do something—

anything.

I need to make

my mark.

I crawl slowly away

from the terrified

cop with the gun

trembling in his hand,

yet I stare.

I stare ahead

with one

single

thought

in my mind:

My future.

I can't lose it.

Yulissa C. Gerard, 14
Morrow, Georgia

30. How I Wish

How I wish I could laugh again,

how I wish I could smile once more,

but instead, I sit and stare at all of my friends while they play even more.

Why do they laugh? I ask.

Why don't they feel the pain I feel?

Do they not know?

Last night, I died on the cold winter street.

By the bullet of grief,

I slowly fall into a deep sleep,

never to wake up in a day or a week.

So cold, but so sweet.

Maybe next time, I could eat.

Sit at the table with my family this week; sure would be sweet.

How I wish I could be.

Chloe Mayor, 12
Atlanta, Georgia

31. I Am a Queen

I am a queen.

I am brown.

I am versatile.

I am gorgeous.

I am confident.

I am a leader.

I am not a follower.

I am unique.

I am a Hebrew Israelite.

I am a queen, and my young life matters.

Kaliyah Smith, 12
Atlanta, Georgia

32. My Life

I love my young life.

Don't take my life, officer.

Can we have peace, please?

Matthew Calhoun, 13
Atlanta, Georgia

33. How's Life Been?

"How's life been?"

"It's been great! I just got a job."

Deep down, he just got a minimum wage job because he's the only Black male.

Confusion.

"How's life been?"

"Great."

I've been living in the projects because everyone thinks that I'm a hoodrat.

"How's life been?"

Depressing,

sad,

and confusing.

Why do they stereotype me?

Duor Duor, 14
Atlanta, Georgia

34. Afros

My hair is different.

My hair expresses me.

I can rock any hairstyle—

I can wear my hair natural,

I can wear an Afro,

I can wear braids!

Raegan Howard, 14
Atlanta, Georgia

35. Equal Rights

Black lives should matter;

there isn't a reason they shouldn't.

By being racist, you make our hearts shatter.

You should treat everyone equally.

Don't mistreat people because of their race.

I wish everyone wouldn't be racist.

People shouldn't be accused of doing something because of their race.

They shouldn't be ashamed of who they are.

Jeremiah Thomas, 12
Atlanta, Georgia

36. Dream

I'm 13 with a dream.
Like MLK, my dreams matter.

Every time Black blood is spilt, the people get sadder.
With my dream, maybe the world can change,
because it's bigger than Black and white.
It's a problem with the whole way of life.
The world is supposed to mix, like batter.
That's why my young Black life matters.

Jacob Person, 13
Jacksonville, Florida

37. Social Injustice

I feel social injustice is unfair and it needs to stop.

It makes me feel unsafe.

It makes me feel like a target is on me and I am never safe because

the people who have to protect me don't like my kind.

Malachi King, 11
Tallahassee, Florida

38. House on a Hill

As the sun shines down on it

in the darkest nights, it stands bright

like a blue giant in the night.

To be the light in someone's life

on this night, it grows bright.

Now, this light of hope can be seen

all over the galaxy.

Hilton McGill, 13
Atlanta, Georgia

39. Jailah's Thoughts

Justice should be for everyone.

All people deserve to be treated equally.

Ignorance will keep us divided.

Love can bring us together.

America can be a better place.

Hope for a better future.

Jailah McCary, 10
Tallahassee, Florida

40. This Is Me

Say it loud:
KEN'NYA!

Keeping calm and being me.
Energized, more than the bunny.
Nosy, this is me.
Neat, that's what I love about me.
Young and fresh are what I will always be.
Adventurous—I know I am, so explore with me!

Say it loud:
THIS IS ME!

Ken'Nya Bevel, 10
Atlanta, Georgia

41. Those Two

Somehow, it's always those two:

black and white,

night and day,

light and dark.

It's always those two who can never seem to prosper as one.

Those whose skin is as dark as night

always have the most scars.

But, just as the warmth of the sun, it never seems to be enough.

There are those whose skin is as light as sun,

who were deemed as precious as gold since their first rise.

Just as the sun, they take,

and take,

and take.

Amaya Conner, 12
Atlanta, Georgia

42. Racism

I think racism is unfair.

If we were treated the same, the

world would be a better place.

I feel like if God made us

like this, you've got to accept that.

If we are racist, that is going to

end the world.

Brisen Bidwin, 11
Tallahassee, Florida

43. Life's Loveliness

My life is important.

My life is good.

My life can sometimes be hard,

like chopping down wood.

Family is important.

Family is everything.

Sometimes, they say things that hurt,

but only so you learn the essential things.

God is good.

God is grace.

He did good things in the past,

but soon, He stopped running,

just like in a race.

Ari Kelly, 11
Atlanta, Georgia

44. I Am...

I am smart.

I am magical.

I am not afraid to speak my mind.

I am brave.

I am free.

I am beautiful.

I am me.

Rhyan Sanders, 11
Baltimore, Maryland

45.) I Wish

I wish for police to treat us right.
I will fight for it with all my might.

I wish for the whites to stop bringing hate,
and this is all because of our race.

I wish for them to stop being unfair.
We can just be happy and try not to compare.

We don't have to get beat walking down the halls.
We will continue to fight to bring justice for all.

Samuel Williams, 12
Atlanta, Georgia

46. Who Am I?

Who Am I?

I am Black.

I am brave.

I am playful.

I am cool.

I am smart.

I am friendly.

I am athletic.

I am creative.

I am a good listener.

I am a good reader.

I am a great person.

I am me.

Jared Earley, 11
Atlanta, Georgia

47. Hate in Their Hearts

I wish police would respect my kind.
Stop giving us all these unnecessary
and hard times.

We've been fighting for freedom for years,
trying to make life better for us and our peers.

They should just be fair and
try not to compare.

I wish the police would stop all their hate,
trying to decide my people's fate.

All the hate in their hearts, just
because of my people's traits.

My fate cannot be decided by
anyone else but myself.

But my people are the greats.
And we create.

Legend Dominguez, 11
Atlanta, Georgia

48. Black for the WIN!

I walk in the store to buy a snack.

I get accused of stealing because I am Black.

I waited one hour to get out of jail.

All the guards were looking at me; my face was pale.

They try to discourage me because of my skin,

but it doesn't work. Black for the WIN!

Mateen Ali, 11
Atlanta, Georgia

49. My Skin

My skin's a great thing!

My skin shows my heritage.

It's why I'm a king!

Joseph (Cruz) Doriney, 12
Atlanta, Georgia

50. Black Life Matters

Be yourself.

Love yourself.

Make a difference.

Achieve.

Thoughtfulness is key.

Trust yourself.

Encourage others.

Reality is amazing.

Succeed and you will make a difference in life.

Bryce Hardwick, 14
Jacksonville, Florida

51. I Am Black and Proud

I am Black and proud.

I say it loud: I am Black and proud.

I am who I say I am.

I love being Black, and I will not take a step back.

I am Black, smart, and kind.

I am one of a kind.

My Black future is bright.

I will achieve because this is what I believe.

I say it loud: I am Black and proud.

Larry B. Edwards III, 17
Jacksonville, Florida

52. If You Like It or Not

I am Black if you like it or not.
No, I won't sit and rot.
Why does freedom have to be fought for?
Why is it harder for us to score?
I am Black if you like it or not.
No, I won't sit and rot.

Joshua Edwards, 12
Tallahassee, Florida

53. My Dream

My dream is precious.
As it goes through, my skin
is the same; it's not different.

Dude, one day, I will say,
"I'm a pilot," too!
You can't judge me;
I'm as cool as dew.

I will fly like the Tuskegee Airmen,
soaring through the sky.
I'm the truth; I am not a lie.

I am different, and I will show
it. I don't want someone to blow
my dream away. And now, you know.

Noah Knowles, 11
Atlanta, Georgia

54. Young Black Man

I am a young Black man

whose dreams are to make it to the big leagues,

whose dreams are to help other people believe in equal rights,

who believes all people should be treated the same,

who believes not just young men should be treated right—

all my Black brothers and sisters deserve equality.

Let's make the world a better place.

Peace!

Calen Wiggins, 15
Jacksonville, Florida

55. Racism in America

Sound the alarm! Scream in the rain!

Violence and disrespect cause my people pain.

As a result of being beaten,

blood runs from my veins.

It's 2022 and nothing's changed.

In broad daylight lynched and tamed—Ahmaud Arbery.

Pursued and blamed—Trayvon Martin.

Stopped and shamed—Philando Castile.

Sound the alarm!

Zamari King, 12
Midway, Florida

56. The Evolution of My Brown Skin

My brown skin is soft.
My brown skin is important.
My brown skin is love.
My brown skin is the skin of a future doctor.
My brown skin wins!

Zuri King, 6
Midway, Florida

57. A Terrible Thing

What I think about racism is:

It's bad for Black people.

Another reason that racism is bad is because Black people are not respected

like other people.

Also, another thing about racism:

It is a terrible thing.

Kenyon Thompson, 10
Tallahassee, Florida

58. As Dark as Can Be

I am small and brave.
I am curious.
I am strange.
I am dark as can be, but that's not all to me.
I am beautiful!
I am me!
I am what people want to be.
Don't you worry 'bout me,
for I am who I am supposed to be.
I am mysterious as the sea,
but as simple as a tree.
I am Black,
and that's a fact.
I am me.

Solomon Charles, 14
Atlanta, Georgia

59. In a Better World

In my imagination, nothing goes wrong.

In my imagination, all the days are beautiful and long.

In my imagination, no one needs to go to school.

In my imagination, no one gets bullied and looks like a fool.

Ayla Doriney, 9
Atlanta, Georgia

60. I Am Powerful

I am Hope Adkins.

I was born on February 15, 2014.

I am seven years old.

I love being myself.

I am powerful.

I love who I am right now.

I love the color of my skin and who I am!

I am Black and filled with love and courage.

                      Hope Adkins, 7
                 Stockbridge, Georgia

61. Mama

Love from one's mother is always great.

All my life, I loved what Mama cooked and baked.

When I'm with her, I can't be hurt.

Her love is better than dessert.

The love she gave made me feel so attached,

but when she left work, she would bend over and break her back,

then come home and act fine

even though she only made nickels and dimes.

Milton Howard, 13
Atlanta, Georgia

62. Brown Skin Girl

I am small.

I am brave.

I am loved.

I am Black.

McKinley Brown, 6
Tallahassee, Florida

63. Brown Skin Boy

I love me.

I get A+s in school.

I deserve justice.

I am awesome and

I feel good.

I do not like to be bad.

Aiden Taylor, 6
Tallahassee, Florida

64. Our Power!

We would not have our rights

if we didn't put up a fight;

if Mrs. Rosa didn't make a fuss

about being in the back of the bus;

if MLK didn't preach

the "I Have a Dream" speech.

If we didn't have a voice,

then we wouldn't have a choice.

We didn't swerve,

and as a result, justice was served.

Because of our dreams,

we were finally freed!

Yosahyes Solomon, 14
Jacksonville, Florida

65. Black Strength

I feel disappointed.

Black people helped white people build cities.

We helped them go to war,

and they treat us

like we tried to kill them.

Langston Glen, 9
Tallahassee, Florida

66. CRAIG

Courageous

Respectful

Awesome

Intelligent

Great

Craig Swain, 12
Tallahassee, Florida

67. KAHLAN

Kind to others

A proud Black man

Happy to be Black

Living life to the fullest

A funny person

No need for racism

Kahlan Daniels, 15
Jacksonville, Florida

68. Black is Great

We are Black.

We are amazing.

Why all the violence and tasing?

We have worked so hard to get where we are.

Our skin shines bright like stars.

We are so smart, and our knowledge stretches far.

Life is short, and it's precious.

Black is great, and I hope you get this message.

Cameron Webbe, 12
Atlanta, Georgia

69. My Feelings on My Skin

My skin is great.

My skin is strong.

My skin makes me proud.

My skin is full of culture.

My skin is what makes me who I am.

God gave me my skin for a reason.

Julius LaRosa III, 13
Jacksonville, Florida

70. BLM

When I think about racism,

I feel angry,

disappointed,

and sad.

I try to not think about it,

but when I watch the news

and it talks about racism,

I go straight to my room.

We have gone through a lot as Black people.

Black people should be treated fairly.

Lives should not be lost in a violent way.

My family is Black,

and we stand for justice in our homes.

Michaela Jones, 13
Tallahassee, Florida

71. Up We Go!

We need to rise up.

We can do this together.

We must still fight on.

Clifton Kirkland Jr., 12
Atlanta, Georgia

72. I Am Loved

I am Black and proud.

I am loved.

I am eight years old—Aliyah.

Aliyah Griffin, 8
Tallahassee, Florida

73. I Am Black

I am playful.

I am careful.

I am funny.

I am smart.

I am strong.

I am Black.

I am.

Jaylen Green, 10
Tallahassee, Florida

74. Pretty Black Flower

I am pretty.
I love my black skin.

I like my skin how it is.
Blackness is beautiful!

August James, 6
Tallahassee, Florida

75. Racism Hurts

When I think about racism, I feel mad.
Racism hurts people—
especially Black people.

When Black people get shot,
all I can think about is
racism
and Black Lives Matter.

Something else I think about
when racism happens is
how sad I feel
for the people
who are
dying.

Zaniyah Johnson, 9
Tallahassee, Florida

76. Being Black Is Awesome

Being Black is awesome to me
because I'm beautiful and pretty.

I still love my brown skin,
even though people judge us
by the color of our skin.

I feel mad
because we are treated differently.
Sometimes, I see kids
on the street
crying,
with no blanket,
no food,
and no clean clothes.

Sometimes, I cry,
but I will try
to make a difference
in my community and world.

Deziraye Burgess, 10
Tallahassee, Florida

77. Black Boy, Black Boy

Black boy, Black boy

He stands there strong, Black boy

Why so sad, Black boy?

Why must the men in white stand above in power while the dark men

below remain in vain, Black boy?

Black boy, Black boy

Ryan Kirkland, 14
Jacksonville, Florida

78. Target

We have targets on our backs.

No one gives us slack just because we are Black.

They kill us for no reason and act like we don't have feelings.

Maybe soon it will be ending, or is it just the beginning?

This is not funny; this is a massacre of murdering.

Shooting churches is not okay, but it will be over one day.

Shawn Edwards, 10
Tallahassee, Florida

79. AFRO

African-American girl:
Fearless, empowered, and gorgeous;
Ready to take on the world.
One and only.

Radriannah Holloway, 12
Atlanta, Georgia

80. Our Voice

My voice,

your voice,

our voice.

The way we stand together,

the way we speak together,

the way we PRAY together.

Our religion.

Our justice.

Our movement.

Our brothers.

Our sisters.

Our race.

Our voice.

Our power.

Solomon Bratton, 14
Atlanta, Georgia

81. I Love Being Black

I love being Black because I can change the world.

I can also try to get us better rights,

so we don't have to get treated like animals anymore.

I also want us all to be equal.

Kameron Slater, 10
Tallahassee, Florida

82. JUDITH: Justice for Everyone

Justice should be a part of everyone's life.

United we should ALL be,

Doing what is right and fair.

In order to be together, we have to believe

The equality should be the same for EVERYONE.

Helping equality grow is the most important thing we can do.

Judith Lara, 12
Atlanta, Georgia

83. DURDEN

Don't give up because of the racists.

Uplift yourself and don't let anyone let you down.

Reality is real, and sometimes, you won't have the best days.

Dreaming of stopping the hate.

Everything you do is great and has purpose.

Nothing you do is negative because God wants you to do it.

Tyrell Durden, 12
Atlanta, Georgia

84. I Have Faith

Hi! I'm Faith.

I love to be in my own skin.

I get to live and play all day—

nothing wrong with being a Black girl!

I love being a Black girl!

Another fact about being a Black girl:

You can love yourself—

fully,

wholeheartedly,

without shame.

Everyone, love yourselves.

Faith Adkins, 10
Atlanta, Georgia

85. Things I've Seen

I've seen many prejudices.

I've seen the George Floyd case.

I've seen things occur in my state.

I've seen the Rayshard Brooks case.

I see how it's JUST US who they hate.

Joshua Adkins, 13
Atlanta, Georgia

86. Hard Work Unlocks Your Talent

Hard work unlocks your talent.

Hard work came from our ancestors.

Hard work keeps our culture going.

Hard work made us who we are.

Hard work is what makes me who I am.

Hard work unlocks your talent.

Glen Spencer III, 12
Atlanta, Georgia

87. I Am Love

I am good.
I am love.
I love strawberries!
I am.

Gabriel Lucas, 6
Tallahassee, Florida

88. I Am Amazing

I am a brown-skinned girl.
I love being Black because my family is Black.
I am loved.
I am amazing.
I am loving.
I am smart.
I am reasonable.
I am nice.
I am respectful.
I am an amazing big sister.
I am social.
I am strong.
I am creative.
I am brave.
I am a great listener.
I am helpful.

Ayanna Norton, 12
Tallahassee, Florida

89. Life

Life is too fragile.

If you don't look up sometimes,

you will miss some things.

Scederick Ethan Lamar Jackson, 11
Atlanta, Georgia

90. Black Is Everything

My young life matters because I can make a difference in my world.

I am Black. Black is beautiful.

So many Black people are successful and do many things that white people wish they could.

I feel like they just do certain stuff to make people mad and upset, and it's unnecessary. My feelings are upset and angry.

Milan Davis, 11
Tallahassee, Florida

91. Young and Black

I am Tyler Cooper.

I love being Black because

we have a strong and creative culture.

Being Black allows me to truly be myself

and know that other Black people support me.

I am a young Black king

and I have big dreams.

I dream of peace.

I dream of no bad police.

I dream of everyone treating other people with love.

Tyler Cooper, 11
Atlanta, Georgia

92. Skin

Black lives matter.

Young Black lives matter.

All of the fighting is because of our skin color.

People who are Black are being treated badly because of their skin color.

We are always judged because of our skin color.

People give us bad looks, as if we killed someone.

Then, we are hurt or killed because of our skin color.

Maharajah Shuman, 12
Jacksonville, Florida

93. Why Does It Matter?

Why does it matter that I am Black?
Why does my skin color matter to others?
Why does my hair type matter?
Why does it matter that my culture is different from yours?

Shouldn't it matter that I am nice?
Shouldn't my actions matter—
not my skin color?
What happened to, "Actions speak louder than words"?
Does that saying not apply because I am Black?

Kylee Thomas, 14
Atlanta, Georgia

94. Black Women

Black women are impeccable

with their big 'fros,

their soothing and comforting voices,

and their good cooking;

with their brown skin

and their foxy attitudes;

with their smart thinking

and their graceful singing.

Who are they?

They are Black women!

Mia Morris, 12
Atlanta, Georgia

95. Being Black

I love being Black.

I love my Black melanin and hair.

I love my culture

and the clothes that I wear.

I love being Black.

I love the life lessons I learn each day.

I love God, whom I call upon and pray to.

I love being Black.

I love the family recipes I receive.

I love being Black.

Being Black is the best part of me!

Joshua Battle, 13
Atlanta, Georgia

96. My Feeling

I feel calm because I don't really do anything.

I just be chilling, and when my friends who are at different schools call me,

I feel happy, but I want to see them face-to-face.

When I see my family, I feel happy because I don't see them that much.

Jessica Austin, 8
Tallahassee, Florida

97. I'm Angry

I'm angry because white police are mean like in slavery. They kill Black people like Trayvon Martin and George Floyd, and still, we help them.

Naheiyma Alabama, 10
Tallahassee, Florida

98. I Will Be the Change

I'm Black.

I can be the change.

I'm different!

I can be the change.

I'm beautiful.

I can be the change.

I'm spectacular!

I can be the change.

I'm what I've been waiting for.

I can be the change.

Jeremiah Adkins, 15
Atlanta, Georgia

99. I Am Not Afraid

I am Filipino.

I am Black.

I am Blackapino.

I am creative.

I am artistic.

I am smart.

I am enthusiastic.

I am scared of failure.

I am scared of a lot of things, but:

I am not afraid of friendship.

I am not afraid to speak up.

I am not afraid to be loud.

I am not afraid of my potential.

Zachary Rodolfo Dennis, 11
Atlanta, Georgia

100. My People

I love Black people.

Black people are loving and kind to the world,

but they treat us like trash.

We will continue to fight on and on.

Everett Price, 13
Tallahassee, Florida

101. I Am Grateful

Who am I?

I am Black.

I am mixed.

Who am I?

I have beautiful hair.

I have nice eyes.

I am grateful for my body.

Who am I?

Who am I?

I am me!

Jayla Ward, 11
Atlanta, Georgia

102. I Love My Hair

I love my hair.

My hair is unique.

I love my hair.

My hair is me.

I love my hair.

My hair is my prized possession.

I love my hair.

I love my hair!

Shakina Powell, 12
Atlanta, Georgia

103. Multifaceted

I'm Black
and beautiful.
I'm Black
and happy.
I'm Black
and educated.
I'm Black
and amazing.
I'm Black
and unique.
I'm Black—
and glad to be.
I'm Black
and handsome.
I'm Black
and grateful.
And, lastly,
I'm Black
and proud.

Jordan Adkins, 11
Atlanta, Georgia

104. Wouldn't You Hate

Wouldn't you hate a world where every day, when you walk outside,

you get yelled at

for the color of your skin?

Every day, I'm late for the bus.

I always have to chase the bus,

just for the white man to stop and let me in.

All of the other kids look at me with disgust

as I walk to the back of the bus.

How I hate this world.

Wouldn't you hate to see

the little Black kids being

shot up or arrested?

When I walk into the school and see the kids being bullied

and pushed into lockers,

I hate it.

If only it could change.

Alaska Lockhart, 13
Atlanta, Georgia

105. The Scared Twelve-Year-Old

It's 12:00 p.m. and I am asleep.

10 minutes later, I am woken up by a loud gasp by my mom.

I run downstairs to see the news on the TV:

A Black man was just suffocated by a white cop.

Just like my mom, I'm in shock.

I am forced to go outside,

although I am scared of the outdoors now.

In the car, I roll the window down.

I see the protest.

I see the protest.

Tristen Patterson, 12
Atlanta, Georgia

106. What Makes Me Special?

My long hair is beautiful.

My brown eyes are pretty.

My voice is gorgeous.

My brown skin is important to me.

I have good ideas.

My smile shines in any room.

My family makes me happy.

I love to grow flowers to see them bloom.

I am special because God made me!

Melody Lewis, 7
Milwaukee, Wisconsin

Antionette Mutcherson, MBA

As a young child, Antionette "Toni" Mutcherson, MBA remembers falling in love with literature. Toni is a product of Hillsborough and Leon County schools in Florida. She credits her mother and schoolteachers for planting the seeds of reading and writing within her as an elementary-age student. Life has come full-circle now that Toni volunteers, facilitates workshops, and speaks at schools across the country. Toni presented a TEDx Talk, "One Mom's Quest to Win Back Her Child from YouTube," in November 2019 on the importance of childhood literacy.

Toni began writing at a young age, and in 2013, she published the first of three children's books in the Adventures of Jett Antoinette book series. The series inspired by her nine-year-old daughter, Jett, includes *Where Does Time Go?*, *The Day the White House Turned Green*, and *Jett Visits Delta Land*. All of her titles have been featured in the Delta Authors on Tour Directory from 2014 to 2018. Toni was motivated to write her third and award-winning title, *Jett Visits Delta Land*, which is the first title under her independent publishing company, BFF Publishing LLC. In June 2019, Toni published her latest title, *How to Secure the Children's Book Bag: An Interactive Guide to Writing, Publishing, and Marketing Children's Books*.

In 2007, Toni graduated from Clark Atlanta University with a bachelor's degree in Business Administration, and in 2017, she received her master's degree in Business Administration from Florida Agricultural and Mechanical University. Toni is an active member of Delta Sigma Theta Sorority, Incorporated. She lives in Atlanta, Georgia.

As an advocate for children's literacy, she lives by the mantra, "Readers are leaders."

To find out more about Antionette "Toni" Mutcherson, visit www.bffpublishinghouse.com.

Riel Felice

Riel Felice graduated from Florida State University in 2020 with a Bachelor of Science degree in Media/Communications Studies and a Bachelor of Arts degree in Editing, Writing, and Media. In addition, Riel was a Spring 2019 initiate into the Kappa Epsilon Chapter of Delta Sigma Theta Sorority, Incorporated. Riel is a professional editor with heavy experience; she has edited numerous books of varying genres, in addition to screenplays, blog posts, magazine articles, social media content, and more. She possesses an unmatched adoration for the written word.

Riel loves to center herself in her spirituality through activities such as yoga and meditation; spend quality time with loved ones; indulge in self-care; enjoy picnics on the beach; and, ultimately, explore and experience the world through eyes that perceive the unconditional love in all things and all people.